Praying Genesis

The Living Word Series

Praying through the Bible, one book at a time.

Praying Genesis

Prayers for Creation, Covenant, and New Beginnings

GRAHAM JOSEPH HILL

Eagna Publishing • Sydney, Australia

PRAYING GENESIS
Prayers for Creation, Covenant, and New Beginnings

Published by: Eagna Publishing (Sydney, Australia)
eagnapublishing@icloud.com
Cover and interior design: Graham Joseph Hill
www.grahamjosephhill.com

paperback isbn: 978-1-7643311-0-4
ebook isbn: 978-1-7643311-1-1
version number 2025-11-07

NATIONAL
LIBRARY
OF AUSTRALIA

A catalogue record for this book is available from the National Library of Australia

Contents

Prologue: Before the Word Was Spoken

Before the Word was spoken,
silence held its breath.
Darkness waited like fertile soil
for light to strike it awake.
And still the Spirit hovers,
over deserts, over cities, over hearts
that long to begin again.
The same voice that shaped the stars
speaks our names from dust,
inviting us to rise,
to build, to bless, to believe.
Each prayer is a seed of that beginning,
small, humble, hopeful, alive.
In praying Genesis,
we remember what we've often forgotten:
that creation isn't finished,
and every breath is a chance
to start again with God.

Introduction: Praying the Beginnings

Genesis isn't only the first book of Scripture; it is the seedbed of the whole story of God. It opens with light and ends with a coffin in Egypt, yet through every beginning and ending runs the same unbroken thread: God's faithfulness. Genesis tells of creation's beauty and human betrayal, of promises made to wanderers, of blessing that keeps pushing through fear, deceit, and famine. It is a book of births and burials, of altars and exiles, of laughter and lament. In these pages, we meet the God who creates, covenants, wrestles, remembers, and redeems. To pray Genesis is to enter the mystery of divine persistence: the love that never gives up on dust.

Praying through Genesis forms us in a different way than studying it alone. Prayer takes truth off the page and places it in our bloodstream. When we pray these ancient stories, we join their characters in awe and failure; we name our own idols, rivalries, and dreams in their light. We discover that every garden, wilderness, and family quarrel echoes in us and in our world. To pray Genesis is to learn how beginnings are always possible again, personally, communally, and cosmically.

These prayers are meant for both solitude and community. They can be read slowly, one chapter at a time, as a companion to Scripture reading; or spoken aloud in worship, study groups, or gatherings seeking renewal. Some readers will pray them as a confession, while others will pray them as an intercession. Each prayer invites engagement rather than performance, an opening of the heart to the God who speaks through stories.

Every prayer follows an intentional pattern shaped by Scripture's own rhythm:

- Invocation: naming God in ways revealed by the passage.

- Confession: acknowledging the distortions in us and our world.
- Lament: grieving what is broken or lost.
- Hope in God: turning the eyes toward divine faithfulness.
- Petition: asking for transformation, justice, and renewal.
- Commitment: pledging to live differently by grace.
- Eschatological Hope: looking toward the world made whole.
- Doxology/Assurance: ending in praise, joy, and trust.

This structure mirrors the movement of the Psalms and the spiritual life itself: from naming, to truth-telling, to sorrow, to hope, to praise. The pattern holds lament and joy together so that neither becomes shallow: the honesty of pain leading us into the freedom of worship.

As you journey through these prayers, pause often. Let specific lines become your own. Insert the names of your community, your city, your wounds. Use silence as part of the conversation; Genesis begins with the Spirit hovering over quiet water. These prayers aren't substitutes for Scripture, but doorways into it: a way to hear the ancient stories breathe again in our century.

Genesis begins in a garden and ends with a promise that carries us toward freedom. It assures us that the God who called light from darkness is still at work: creating, reconciling, and blessing through ordinary people who dare to believe. May these prayers teach us to see the world as Genesis sees it: unfinished, beloved, and always on the verge of new creation.

Let There Be Light Again (Genesis 1)

Creator of light and land,
>Lover of humanity and all creation,
>you who spoke order from chaos,
>you who declared goodness over every creature,
>we bring before you this fractured world.

The earth reels beneath heat and flood,
>forests gasp, rivers choke, skies thicken with smoke.

Children are hungry while tables overflow with waste.

Bombs fall on cities, leaders trade lies,
>migrants wander without welcome,
>and neighbors scorn one another in fear and rage.

We name it before you,
>our greed, our violence, our indifference,
>and we confess: this isn't the world you called "very good."

Yet you're still the One who hovers over deep waters,
>still the One who separates dark from light,
>still the One who blesses creation with abundance and beauty.

Speak again, O God.

Divide despair from hope.

Separate cruelty from justice.

Call forth life where death has reigned too long.

Stir us into your image once more:
>to tend the soil instead of strip it,
>to welcome strangers instead of banishing them,
>to honor truth instead of weaponizing it,
>to share bread and guard dignity,

to love mercy and walk humbly in your presence.
You made us in your image and call us beloved,
> may we love like you,
> show mercy and grace,
> do justice in your way,
> be peacemakers as your children,
> reflect your righteousness and holiness,
> and tend your earth with care.

We ache for your Sabbath rest,
> where all may flourish,
> where lion and lamb, worker and owner, refugee and ruler
> find peace side by side.

Don't let us settle for darkness.
Command again, "Let there be light,"
> and make us bearers of that dawn.

Blessed are you, Light of the world,
> who shines in the darkness,
> and the darkness can't overcome you.

Blessed are you, Creator of sun and stars,
> who gives warmth to the earth and beauty to the skies.

Blessed are you, Christ our dawn,
> who scatters night and leads us into day.

Even now, your radiance rises.
Even now, your glory breaks forth.
Even now, your Spirit kindles hope within us.
Amen.

Breath into Dust (Genesis 2)

Breath of Life,

    you who stooped to dust,

    you who formed humanity with tender hands,

    you who breathed your own Spirit into clay,

    hear us now.

We're the soil you called good,

    yet we scar the ground with greed.

We're gardeners of Eden,

    yet we strip forests bare,

    pollute rivers,

    treat the earth as a commodity,

    not communion.

You planted a garden for delight and care,

    yet our cities choke with smoke,

    our laborers toil without rest,

    our families fracture,

    our neighbors are cast aside.

We confess:

    we have forgotten the gift of breath,

    the dignity of bodies,

    the holy calling to tend and keep.

But you, O Lord of every garden,

    still walk among us in the cool of the day.

Still, you whisper through the trees,

    still, you offer living water,

    still, you invite us to Sabbath rest,

still, you call us beloved and call us to care for your creation.
So, breathe again.
Breathe justice where lungs collapse under war's smoke.
Breathe mercy where workers collapse under endless hours.
Breathe peace where hatred poisons communities.
Breathe courage where fear has stolen voice.
Shape us again from the ground of your mercy.
Plant in us seeds of generosity,

> water us with grace,
> till our lives may yield fruit for healing,
> shade for the weary,
> bread for those who hunger,
> love for your earth,
> care for your plant,
> compassion for humanity.

You join us with those whom we love,

> may they be bone of our bone,
> flesh of our flesh,
> recipients and givers of love,
> and may our unity reflect your divine love.

Let us be soil where your Spirit dwells,

> human and holy together,
> dust and breath,
> servants and beloved,
> in the name of Jesus,
> the Word made flesh,

Blessed are you, Breath of Life,

> who fills every creature with spirit and song.

Blessed are you, Gardener of Eden,

> who makes deserts bloom and hearts rejoice.

Blessed are you, Christ our rest,

> who offers living water to the weary.

Even now, you breathe upon dry bones.

Even now, you plant hope in barren soil.
Even now, your Spirit makes us new.
Amen.

Hiding and Hope (Genesis 3)

God of the garden,
> you who walked among trees and rivers,
> you who sought us when we hid in shame,
> hear our cry.

We confess we have grasped for what isn't ours,
> trusted lies more than your love,
> and covered ourselves in fear and pride.

We have hidden from you,
> and in hiding, we have wounded one another
> and stripped your earth bare.

Our voices echo with excuses,
> our systems trade in deceit,
> our leaders grasp for power,
> our marketplaces worship greed.

We feel the thorns of violence and the sweat of endless toil.

We see exile written on the faces of refugees,
> alienation carved into neighborhoods,
> estrangement planted in families.

The ground is cursed because of our sin,
> our childbearing pains are severe,
> our relationships with each other and the earth are broken,
> we toil all the days of our lives,
> from dust we were formed and to dust we return,
> and we're banished from Eden.

Yet you're the God who still calls,
> "Where are you?"

You clothe the ashamed,

> you set a promise of deliverance,

> you restore relationships,

> you plant seeds of hope in cursed soil,

> you make a healing way through your Son.

So, call us out of hiding.

> Strip away our false coverings.

Teach us to walk again in your presence,

> to tend creation with reverence,

> to live reconciled with one another,

> to trust the One who crushes the serpent.

Let mercy be our covering,

> love our guiding star,

> and justice our way home.

Blessed are you, God who seeks the hidden,

> for your mercy clothes our shame.

Blessed are you, Christ our deliverer,

> for your heel crushes the serpent and your cross opens Eden's gate.

Blessed are you, Spirit of hope,

> for you plant new creation in weary soil.

Even now, your voice calls us beloved.

Even now, your grace restores what was lost.

Even now, your promise leads us home.

Amen.

Blood in the Soil (Genesis 4)

God who listens to cries from the ground,
> you who saw the hand that rose in violence,
> you who asked, "Where is your sibling?",
> hear us.
We confess the envy that corrodes our hearts,
> the rivalries that fracture our communities,
> the hatred that spills into streets and nations.
Blood cries out from the earth:
> from war zones and prisons,
> from neighborhoods marked by poverty,
> from homes torn by rage.
We justify ourselves,
> we turn away,
> we refuse to be our sibling's keeper.
Yet you still mark us with mercy,
> still send us eastward with protection,
> still call us to repentance and return.
God of the restless wanderer,
> till our hearts until they yield compassion.
Break our cycles of revenge.
Teach us to guard one another's dignity,
> to build cities of justice rather than violence,
> to offer gifts born of gratitude, not competition.
Let reconciliation rise where blood has stained.
Let mercy speak louder than vengeance.
Let your Spirit keep us,

so that we may keep one another.

Blessed are you, Keeper of all life,

for you hear the blood that cries from the ground.

Blessed are you, Christ of mercy,

for your blood speaks a better word than vengeance.

Blessed are you, Spirit of reconciliation,

for you break hostility and sow peace.

Even now, your grace marks us for life.

Even now, your promise gathers the scattered.

Even now, your love makes us siblings again.

Amen.

Generations of Dust and Breath (Genesis 5)

Ancient One,

> you who bless generations,
>
> you who remember every name,
>
> you who keep covenant through ages long forgotten,
>
> hear us.

We confess we treat life as disposable,

> we reduce names to numbers,
>
> we erase those experiencing poverty from memory,
>
> we exalt the powerful as if they were gods.

Our histories are written by victors,

> our family lines fractured by greed,
>
> our children inherit violence, not blessing.

We lament the brevity of our days,

> the shadow of death that haunts us,
>
> the despair of generations who see no future.

We grieve the weight of legacies:

> slavery and conquest,
>
> colonial wounds and economic chains,
>
> the sins of ancestors that still scar the soil.

Yet you're the God who remembers,

> who walks with the righteous,
>
> who carries Enoch into your presence,
>
> who breathes promise through lineages,
>
> who brings forth hope even through weary wombs.

So, renew us, Lord of every generation.

Teach us to number our days in wisdom.

Let us write histories of mercy,

    let us bear legacies of justice,

    let us hand on blessings not curses.

Mark us with your Spirit,

    so that our lives may echo faith,

    our families reflect your love,

    our communities carry your covenant,

    our children inherit your peace.

Until death is no more

    and every name is remembered in your kingdom,

    we trust your promise through all generations.

Blessed are you, Ancient of Days,

    for your faithfulness spans every generation.

Blessed are you, Christ our life,

    for in you death is swallowed up and hope made new.

Blessed are you, Spirit of promise,

    for you write mercy into our names and futures.

Even now, you walk with us as you walked with Enoch.

Even now, you carry weary lineages into grace.

Even now, you make our dust shine with your breath.

Amen.

Corruption and Covenant (Genesis 6)

God of grieving heart,
>you who looked upon the earth and saw its violence,
>you who mourned the corruption of flesh and soil,
>you who chose mercy even in judgment,
>hear us.

We confess the violence of our hands,
>the schemes of our empires,
>the arrogance of our technologies,
>the idolatry of our artificial intelligence,
>the cruelty of our economies.

We build weapons faster than bread,
>we exploit creation without reverence,
>we treat your image-bearers as expendable.

We lament a world filled with bloodshed:
>children displaced by war,
>oceans choked with plastic,
>nations drowning in greed.

The cries of the oppressed rise like floodwaters,
>and we feel the weight of your sorrow.

Yet you are the God who remembers Noah,
>the God who plants seeds of covenant,
>the God who holds back chaos for the sake of life.

Even in wrath, you set your face toward redemption.

So, teach us to walk with you,
>to be blameless in corrupt days,
>to build arks of hospitality and justice,

to preserve life with courage and faith.
Mark us with your covenant promise,
> so that in an age of ruin we may be signs of mercy,
> so that in a culture of violence we may sow peace,
> so that in a flood of despair we may bear hope.
Until your new creation dawns,
> and righteousness dwells upon the earth,
> we walk with you.
Blessed are you, Covenant-Keeper,
> for your mercy is wider than the flood.
Blessed are you, Christ our ark,
> for in you we are carried through the waters of death to life.
Blessed are you, Spirit of renewal,
> for you brood over chaos and birth creation again.
Even now, your bow of promise bends across the sky.
Even now, your faithfulness steadies the earth.
Even now, your love preserves a remnant of hope.
Amen.

Shut In by Mercy (Genesis 7)

God of flood and ark,
      you who open the fountains of the deep,
      you who shut the door to preserve life,
      you who remember covenant even in storm,
      hear us.
We confess the corruption of our days:
      we have polluted seas,
      we have exalted violence as strength,
      we have mocked your patience,
      we have built towers of greed and called them progress.
We deny our dependence on you,
      and our idols can't save.
We lament a world drowning in sorrow:
      cities submerged by rising seas,
      nations torn by endless war,
      those experiencing poverty swept away
            while the powerful find refuge.
      The cries of creation are a deluge in your ears,
      and the earth groans beneath our ruin.
Yet you, O Lord, remember mercy.
You appoint an ark of salvation.
You keep covenant through rain and rising waters.
You hold life in your hands until the storm subsides.
So, gather us into your refuge.
Seal us with your Spirit.
Teach us to preserve life with reverence,

to build communities that shelter the vulnerable,

to resist despair with hope.

Make us witnesses of covenant,

bearers of your promise in an age of flood,

guardians of creation's dignity,

disciples who walk with you through storm and stillness.

Until the waters recede,

until new creation rises,

until righteousness dwells upon the earth,

keep us steadfast in faith.

Blessed are you, God of the rainbow,

for your mercy is stronger than wrath.

Blessed are you, Christ our ark,

for you carry us through death into life.

Blessed are you, Spirit of renewal,

For even now you prepare dry ground beneath our feet.

Amen.

When the Waters Recede (Genesis 8)

God who remembers,
>you who shut in with mercy and open the earth again,
>you who send a dove across the waters,
>you who whisper hope on the wind,
>hear us.

We confess our impatience in waiting,
>our fear when storms don't quickly end,
>our despair when waters linger too long.

We grasp for control,
>we distrust your timing,
>we forget your covenant love.

We lament the floods that drown creation still:
>islands lost to rising seas,
>homes washed away in storms,
>communities stranded in despair.

We cry with those who wait for dry ground,
>for the end of exile,
>for the return of peace.

Yet you are the God who remembers Noah,
>who opens the fountains of mercy,
>who makes a new beginning where all seemed lost.

So, open the windows of our hearts.

Let faith take flight like a dove.

Teach us to wait with patience,
>to trust your timing,
>to rejoice in the first green shoot of renewal.

Make us guardians of life,
  builders of peace,
  caretakers of creation,
  people who carry hope into the ruins.
Until the whole earth is dry again,
  until every exile finds home,
  until death itself recedes,
  we look for your new creation.
Blessed are you, Lord of the winds and waters,
  for you remember mercy in every storm.
Blessed are you, Christ our refuge,
  for you open the door to a new beginning.
Blessed are you, Spirit of life,
  for you brood over chaos until peace is born.
Amen.

Bow in the Clouds (Genesis 9)

God of covenant,
>
> you who set a rainbow as your promise,
>
> you who bind yourself to creation with mercy,
>
> you who remember every creature,
>
> hear us.

We confess our breaking of covenant:

> our treaties betrayed,
>
> our promises abandoned,
>
> our words emptied of truth.

We fracture community,

> we exploit creation,
>
> we forget the God who swears never to forsake.

We lament the violence that still floods the earth:

> wars that drench the soil in blood,
>
> nations arming for destruction,
>
> families broken by betrayal.

We mourn that we still live as if there were no covenant,

> as if your rainbow were a fading dream.

Yet you are the God who remembers,

> who hangs your bow in the clouds,
>
> who lays down weapons of wrath,
>
> who binds yourself to life.

So, mark us with your covenant.

Teach us to be people of promise,

> keepers of peace,
>
> caretakers of creation.

Let our lives be rainbows of mercy,

>signs that violence won't prevail.

Make us covenant-bearers in this age:

>steadfast in truth,

>bold in reconciliation,

>faithful in justice,

>merciful in love.

Until every tear is dried,

>until sword becomes plow,

>until the earth is filled with your glory,

>we will live as children of your covenant.

Blessed are you, O God of promise,

>for your mercy stretches from generation to generation.

Blessed are you, Christ our peace,

>for your cross is the rainbow of new creation.

Blessed are you, Spirit of life,

>for even now you seal us with grace.

Amen.

Table of Nations (Genesis 10)

God of every tribe and tongue,
>you who scatter peoples and weave them into families of earth,
>you who delight in difference,
>you who bless nations with abundance,
>hear us.

We confess the pride that exalts one people over another,
>the fear that builds walls,
>the greed that hoards land and wealth.

We erase histories not our own,
>we exploit cultures for profit,
>we despise the stranger you call beloved.

We lament the divisions that scar the human family:
>wars of ethnicity and race,
>colonial wounds still festering,
>the hatred that fuels nationalism.

We mourn that your table of nations is a battlefield instead of a feast.

Yet you are the God who blesses families of the earth,
>who promises life to every tribe,
>who calls us kin through your covenant of grace.

So, teach us to honor every culture,
>to rejoice in every language,
>to celebrate diversity as your gift.

Make us builders of bridges,
>hosts of welcome,
>disciples of reconciliation.

Mark us as your children,

called not to dominate but to serve,
not to exclude but to embrace,
not to curse but to bless.

Until every nation gathers at your throne,
until every tongue sings your praise,
until the earth is filled with your glory,
keep us faithful.

Blessed are you, God of the nations,
for your mercy embraces all peoples.

Blessed are you, Christ our peace,
for you break down every dividing wall.

Blessed are you, Spirit of unity,
for you make one family from many.

Amen.

Tower of Pride (Genesis 11)

God who confuses arrogant plans,
    you who scatter the proud,
    you who resist empires,
    you who draw near to the humble,
    hear us.
We confess the towers we build:
    skyscrapers of greed,
    technologies of control,
    empires of domination.
We trust in our own name,
    we worship progress as salvation,
    we forget the God who made us dust.
We lament a world chasing Babel's dream:
    languages silenced,
    cultures erased,
    communities bent to one will.
We mourn economies that grind those experiencing poverty,
    technologies that surveil and enslave,
    politics that worship power.
Yet you are the God who comes down,
    who disrupts arrogance,
    who scatters pride,
    who preserves difference as gift.
So, humble us, O Lord.
Confuse our idols.
Turn our towers into temples of mercy.

Teach us to bear your name, not our own,
  to build not monuments but communities of justice.
Mark us with your Spirit,
  that we may be a people of Pentecost:
  diverse yet united,
  many voices yet one song,
  all proclaiming your glory.
Until the nations are healed,
  until every tower falls,
  until the city of God descends,
  we will walk in your way.
Blessed are you, Judge of nations,
  for you cast down the proud.
Blessed are you, Christ our cornerstone,
  for you build a house of living stones.
Blessed are you, Spirit of fire,
  For you make many tongues one praise.
Amen.

Called to Leave, Called to Bless (Genesis 12)

God who speaks into ordinary days with disruptive grace,
>you call us to go:
>to leave what is familiar,
>to trust promises we can't yet see,
>to believe that blessing isn't for hoarding but for giving.

We confess how easily we shrink back.
We cling to safety,
>we build shrines to comfort,
>we chase dreams of prosperity while ignoring your call.

We want the fruit of your promise
>without the risk of your journey.

And we lament:
>whole nations barricading themselves behind walls,
>families torn from their lands,
>the poor crushed under the weight of others' abundance.

The blessing you promised for every family of the earth
>too often looks like privilege for the few.

Yet still you call,
>still, you promise,
>still, you lead wanderers into wide, unknown lands.

So, send us again.
Break our grip on what is small and safe.
Give us courage to step into the wilderness of trust,
>to bless those who curse,
>to build communities of mercy and hospitality.

We will walk with you until the promise swells to fullness,

until every family is gathered in joy,

until the nations rejoice in your blessing.

Blessed are you, Faithful One,

who calls us beyond ourselves

and makes us pilgrims of hope.

Amen.

Altars and Open Hands (Genesis 13)

God of quiet fields and open skies,
> you hold the land in your hands
> and teach us that peace matters more than property.

We confess the rivalries that consume us:
> families split over inheritance,
> neighbors feuding over boundaries,
> nations warring for soil and oil.

We grasp for what looks good to the eyes,
Forgetting that your promise can't be measured in acres.
We lament a world scarred by greed:
> rivers poisoned for profit,
> villages emptied for mines,
> lands stolen and called conquest.

We mourn how easily we trade kinship for gain.
Yet you speak again, renewing promise.
You tell us to lift our eyes,
> to see expanses we can't count,
> to trust that your blessing is bigger than rivalry.

So, teach us to yield when strife arises,
> to choose peace over possession,
> to build altars instead of empires.

Let generosity be our witness,
> and reconciliation our inheritance.

We will walk in trust until the earth is healed,
> until your children dwell together without fear,
> until every promise finds its rest in you.

Blessed are you, Giver of the land,

> for your promise can't be contained by fences.

Amen.

Bread and Wine in the Valley (Genesis 14)

God Most High,

    possessor of heaven and earth,

    you meet us not in triumphal halls

    but in the valley of battle-weariness,

    with bread to steady us

    and wine to gladden our hearts.

We confess how often we worship power.

We bow to kings who promise security,

    we chase victories that leave others ruined,

    we grasp spoils we did not earn.

Too easily we imagine might as blessing,

    and forget the One who gives life itself.

We lament a world addicted to conquest:

    streets littered with the debris of war,

    families uprooted for someone else's profit,

    whole nations treated as bargaining chips.

We ache for those trampled underfoot,

    their stories erased from the ledgers of empire.

Yet even here you send Melchizedek,

    a priest who blesses in your name,

    who reminds us that true strength

    comes not from swords or treaties

    but from your mercy.

So, teach us to resist the seduction of plunder,

    to turn away from the bribes of kings,

    to live with open hands,

receiving bread as gift and wine as grace.
Let us become altars in the midst of strife,
    people whose lives point beyond empire
    to your kingdom of peace.
Until every valley is lifted,
    until justice and mercy sit together at the table,
    until swords are remembered no more,
    we look for your blessing.
Blessed are you, God Most High,
    who delivers the vulnerable,
    who feeds the weary,
    who blesses the peacemaker.
Amen.

Stars Beyond Number (Genesis 15)

God of covenant,
> you take us outside our tents of fear,
>
> bid us look up,
>
> and count the stars:
>
> a promise too vast to hold,
>
> yet spoken with tenderness.

We confess our doubts.

We demand proofs and contracts,
> we waver when the waiting grows long,
>
> we measure your faithfulness by our timetables.

Too often we settle for small dreams
> because trust feels too costly.

We lament the shadows that threaten promise:
> infertile fields and empty cradles,
>
> systems that smother the poor,
>
> hopes deferred until hearts grow sick.

We mourn how promises are broken:
> by leaders, by nations, by ourselves,
>
> leaving generations wounded.

Yet you step into the night,
> cut covenant in your own blood,
>
> and pledge yourself to us
>
> even when we falter.

So, steady our trembling hearts.

Teach us to wait in hope,
> to trust when evidence is thin,

to believe that your word
is more enduring than fear.
Make us people who live as heirs of promise,
carriers of blessing,
pilgrims of faith.
Until every tear is dried,
until the stars are gathered,
until your promise is fulfilled,
we hold fast to your word.
Blessed are you, God of the covenant,
who counts our faith as righteousness.
Blessed are you, Christ our assurance,
whose cross seals the promise.
Blessed are you, Spirit of hope,
who makes us children of Abraham's faith.
Amen.

The God Who Sees (Genesis 16)

God who bends low in the wilderness,
> you hear the cries of the mistreated,
> you see the tears of the forgotten,
> you name the ones cast aside.

We confess our complicity in the stories of Hagar.
We have used power to wound,
> treated people as means to an end,
> justified exploitation in the name of promise.

We have told ourselves we are righteous
> while silencing the voices of those who suffer.

We lament the countless Hagars of our world:
> women forced into labor without dignity,
> migrants fleeing violence with no welcome,
> children born into systems stacked against them.

Their cries rise to heaven,
> and the wilderness bears witness against us.

Yet you are the God who sees.
You find Hagar by a spring of water.
You call her by name,
> you promise life where others decreed despair.

You give her courage to return,
> not as invisible, but as seen, heard, and held.

So, meet us by our springs.
Open our eyes to the ones we have ignored.
Let us be a people who see as you see,
> who refuse to turn away,

who lift the lowly and shelter the vulnerable.
Shape us to be communities
>   where no Hagar is cast out,
>   where every child is cherished,
>   where dignity is guarded like treasure.
Until the wilderness blossoms,
>   until the oppressed sing of freedom,
>   until your mercy makes all things new,
>   we will follow your seeing love.
Blessed are you, Living One who sees me,
>   for you gather the abandoned,
>   you dignify the forgotten,
>   you make life spring up in barren places.
Amen.

Marked for Covenant (Genesis 17)

God Almighty,
>you speak into old age and impossible promise,
>you rename the weary,
>you seal love not with words alone but with flesh and blood.

We confess how lightly we hold covenant.
We make vows we don't keep,
>we love without endurance,
>we treat faith as convenience rather than calling.

We crave your blessing
>but resist the wounding that makes it real.

We lament a world allergic to commitment,
>contracts without loyalty,
>communities fractured by suspicion,
>relationships discarded when they demand sacrifice.

We mourn how belonging has become a brand
>and faithfulness a rarity.

Yet you are the God who cuts covenant in mercy.
You mark your people,
>not for domination but for devotion,
>not to exclude but to remind us that we are yours.

You rename Sarai and Abram with laughter on your breath,
>and promise life where bodies say "impossible."

So, inscribe your faithfulness upon our hearts.
Circumcise our pride,
>our indifference,
>our fear of surrender.

Teach us to bear in our bodies the sign of grace,
to live as those set apart for compassion and justice.
Let our communities become living covenants,
wounds healed into witness,
boundaries turned to belonging,
promises kept in tenderness.
Until all creation bears your name,
until every exile knows they are chosen,
until joy and obedience walk hand in hand,
keep us faithful to your promise.
Blessed are you, God of everlasting covenant,
who gives new names and new beginnings.
Blessed are you, Christ our seal,
whose body bears the wound of love.
Blessed are you, Spirit of promise,
who writes your law upon our hearts.
Amen.

Laughter at the Door (Genesis 18)

God who comes unannounced beneath the oaks,
>who sits down to eat bread still warm from the fire,
>who laughs with the barren and blesses the waiting,
>we welcome you.

We confess how narrow our tents have become.
We ration our hospitality,
>we protect our schedules more fiercely than our neighbors,
>we doubt that anything new could grow from what feels spent.

We smile politely at your promises
>but inwardly shake our heads.

We lament the weariness that makes us cynical,
>the long prayers unanswered,
>the justice deferred,
>the wounds that seem to mock faith.

We grieve a world that closes its doors
>to strangers, migrants, and angels in disguise.

Yet you are the guest who turns host.
You promise life to those who've forgotten how to hope.
You breathe laughter into old lungs,
>and turn disbelief into delight.

So, widen our thresholds,
>soften our skepticism,
>teach us to knead hope into daily bread
>and to meet you in those who arrive hungry or unknown.

Let our tables become altars of grace,
>our laughter a sign of faith reborn,

our lives a witness that nothing is too hard for you.
Until every barren heart conceives joy,
> until every stranger is welcomed home,
> until your laughter fills the whole earth,
> keep us watching by the door.
Blessed are you, God of promise fulfilled,
> who turns cynicism to song.
Blessed are you, Christ our guest and giver,
> who breaks bread with the weary.
Blessed are you, Spirit of joy,
> who fills our tents with holy laughter.
Amen.

Mercy in the Ashes (Genesis 19)

God who weeps over burning cities,
>who sends messengers to warn,
>who grieves before judging,
>who leads the bewildered by the hand,
>we look to you.

We confess that we have loved the glitter of Sodom.
We've built our pleasures on the backs of others,
>we've normalized cruelty for comfort,
>we've turned justice into a bargaining chip.

Even as the sky darkens,
>we hesitate to leave what enslaves us.

We lament a world aflame:
>cities consumed by greed,
>people commodified and discarded,
>the vulnerable trampled in the name of freedom.

We mourn that our societies prize luxury over compassion,
>and that our own hearts too easily turn back.

Yet you are the God who still remembers Lot,
>who drags the reluctant toward safety,
>who preserves a remnant for hope.

Even amid judgment, your mercy smolders like an ember in the dust.
So, lead us out, O Lord.
Pull us from the cities of our own making.
Give us courage to walk without glancing back,
>to trust that what you destroy is what was destroying us.

Teach us to live as people rescued,

to build communities of shelter not indulgence,

to remember that grace is never cheap,

and that holiness is love's fierce protection.

Until the ruins are restored,

until tears are wiped away,

until righteousness shines like morning after smoke,

keep us faithful to your mercy.

Blessed are you, Judge who is also Deliverer,

who remembers even the hesitant.

Blessed are you, Christ our refuge,

who enters the fire to save.

Blessed are you, Spirit of renewal,

who brings beauty from the ash.

Amen.

Truth in the Shadows (Genesis 20)

God of truth and mercy,

    you see through every disguise,

    you protect the innocent from deceit,

    you guard your promise even when your people lose courage.

We confess the half-truths we tell to survive.

We hide behind clever words,

    manipulate stories to protect our image,

    and call it wisdom when it's fear.

We trust our strategies more than your faithfulness.

We lament the harm our evasions cause,

    trust fractured, relationships poisoned,

    innocents drawn into our compromises.

We grieve a world where lies are currency,

    where power rewards the cunning

    and punishes the honest.

Yet you, O Lord, still intervene.

You confront kings in their dreams,

    you shelter the vulnerable from deceit,

    you turn even our failures into moments of mercy.

Your covenant doesn't collapse when we falter,

    your promise outlasts our duplicity.

So, teach us to live unmasked.

Give us courage to tell the truth even when it costs us.

Let integrity become our shelter,

    and humility our strength.

May our words heal instead of wound,

and our lives bear witness to your trustworthiness.
Mark us as people whose speech reflects your light,
      whose honesty restores what fear has broken,
      whose courage invites reconciliation.
Until deceit is no more,
      until nations speak truth without fear,
      until every tongue confesses your faithfulness,
      keep us walking in the light of your promise.
Blessed are you, God of truth,
      who protects even the fearful.
Blessed are you, Christ our integrity,
      whose word is steadfast and whose mercy endures.
Blessed are you, Spirit of holiness,
      who turns confession into new creation.
Amen.

Laughter and Tears (Genesis 21)

God who keeps impossible promises,
>you bring laughter out of barrenness,
>you turn silence into song,
>you remember both the rejoicing and the rejected.

We confess how easily we forget mercy once joy arrives.
We protect our blessings like possessions,
>we defend privilege as if it were divine right.

We forget those pushed to the margins
>by the very promises that comfort us.

We lament the cries in the wilderness,
Hagar's sobs, the child's parched voice,
>the ache of all who are exiled so another might inherit.

We grieve that our rejoicing so often requires another's sorrow,
>that nations still build their prosperity on the suffering of others.

Yet you, O God, hear both laughter and lament.
You open Sarah's womb and Hagar's eyes.
You aren't contained by our boundaries of blessing.
Your covenant overflows the tents of the chosen.
So, teach us to rejoice without exclusion,
>to celebrate gifts without forgetting the outcast,
>to trust that your abundance is wide enough for all.

Let our laughter be humble,
>our joy compassionate,
>our blessings shared.

Make us midwives of promise and guardians of mercy,
>people who nourish hope in every wilderness.

Until all children are fed,

> until every exile finds home,

> until laughter and justice dwell together,

> keep us faithful to your promise of life.

Blessed are you, God who hears every cry,

> who fills barren hearts with joy and dry wells with water.

Blessed are you, Christ our compassion,

> whose mercy embraces the forgotten.

Blessed are you, Spirit of joy,

> who turns both tears and laughter into praise.

Amen.

The Mountain of Mercy (Genesis 22)

God who tests and provides,
>   you call us to places we never wished to go,
>   you speak into the silence of surrender,
>   you lead us up mountains we don't understand.

We confess how easily we mistake fear for faith.
We build altars to our own ambitions,
>   we sacrifice others to secure our future,
>   we cling to certainty instead of trust.

Too often, our zeal wounds the innocent,
>   and our religion hides cruelty in its robes.

We lament every altar of violence:
>   children caught in wars and ideologies,
>   the poor offered up to greed,
>   the earth scorched for profit.

We mourn the ways we use your name
>   to justify the unthinkable.

Yet you, O Lord, call our names twice.
You stay our trembling hands.
You provide what we could never give,
>   a ram caught in mercy's thicket,
>   a substitute born of grace, not fear.

So, teach us to listen for your second word,
>   to see provision where we expected loss,
>   to believe that obedience isn't destruction
>   but the trust that love still holds.

Let our faith become gentle,

our worship life-giving,

    our hands open rather than raised.

Make us witnesses to the God who provides,

    not takers in the name of devotion.

Until the mountain yields peace,

    until sacrifice gives way to compassion,

    until your love is known in every land,

    we will walk and worship.

Blessed are you, God of the ram and the rescue,

    who turns terror into testimony.

Blessed are you, Christ our offering,

    who ends the need for blood.

Blessed are you, Spirit of mercy,

    who teaches our trembling hearts to trust.

Amen.

A Field for Tears (Genesis 23)

God of the living and the dead,
>you watched your Son suffer and die,
>you know what it is to grieve,
>to walk the edge between promise and loss,
>to walk beside us,
>as we honor the bodies and lives of those we love.

We confess how uncomfortable we are with mourning.
We rush past gravesides,
>we measure worth by productivity instead of presence,
>we treat death as failure rather than doorway.

We imagine our lives will continue on this earth,
Instead of living in the light of our mortality.
We forget that love's truest language is lament.
We lament the many who die unseen,
>the aged left alone,
>the nameless buried without witness,
>the victims of war and neglect,
>the land itself scarred and unwept.
>We ache for those whose grief is dismissed,
>whose sorrow finds no home.

Yet you are the God who sanctifies sorrow.
You let Abraham weep without shame.
You grant him land not as conquest, but as burial ground,
>a promise kept through the tenderness of loss.

So, teach us to weep well.
Help us to remember without despair,

to honor the dead by living justly,

to see that mourning is part of faith,

that even tears can water hope.

Let our cemeteries become gardens of resurrection,

our memories seeds of gratitude,

our grief the soil where love endures.

Until the day when death is swallowed by life,

when every tomb becomes empty,

and joy stands where sorrow once knelt,

keep us steadfast in holy remembrance.

Blessed are you, Keeper of our dust,

who holds every name in compassion.

Blessed are you, Christ of tears,

who enters every tomb to bring life.

Blessed are you, Spirit of comfort,

who breathes peace into our mourning.

Blessed are you, Crucified and Resurrected Lord Jesus,

who died and rose again,

that we may also rise to life eternal.

Amen.

At the Well of Promise (Genesis 24)

God who guides the seeking heart,
    you send your messengers on long roads,
    you lead the weary to water,
    you weave providence through ordinary kindness.
We confess our impatience with your timing.
We demand signs on our terms,
    we hurry your purposes,
    we doubt that love could still be your chosen language.
We trust calculation more than prayer,
    and forget that your will is often revealed in the small gesture,
    a cup offered, a word of welcome, a heart that listens.
We lament how easily we make relationships transactional:
    people reduced to utility,
    marriage traded for status,
    covenant thinned into convenience.
We mourn a world suspicious of trust
    and uncertain of love's endurance.
Yet you, O Lord, are the arranger of holy meetings.
You direct the servant's steps,
    you stir generosity in Rebekah's heart,
    you bless the encounter that will carry your promise forward.
So, teach us to notice your divine choreography.
Keep our hearts open to strangers and serendipity.
Let us meet your won't in spectacle but in service,
    not in control but in surrender.
Make our lives wells of refreshment,

places where the thirsty find welcome,

where generosity becomes prayer,

and where promise takes flesh again.

Until every journey ends in blessing,

until love's faithfulness restores the earth,

until your covenant flows through every home,

keep us attentive to your leading.

Blessed are you, God of the well and the road,

who guides the willing and surprises the doubtful.

Blessed are you, Christ our companion,

whose kindness draws us home.

Blessed are you, Spirit of providence,

who writes grace into every encounter.

Amen.

Generations and Thresholds (Genesis 25)

God of the long story,
God of generations past and living,

you gather the living and the dead into your mercy,
you bring new generations to birth

even as the old are gathered home.

You are the keeper of promises across centuries,

the breath within every lineage of faith.

We confess how easily we forget the past.
We cut ourselves off from the wisdom of our elders,

we repeat their mistakes with new pride,

we treat inheritance as possession instead of trust.

We hurry to the next chapter without gratitude for what has been.
We allow rivalry, ego, and ambition to cloud our imaginations,

and degrade our spirits and relationships.

We lament how rivalry divides families still,

siblings turned to enemies,

inheritances that become battlegrounds,

the favoritism that poisons love.

We mourn how easily blessing becomes competition,

how we clutch what was meant to be shared,

how we compare, compete, and hurt each other.

Yet you, O Lord, are faithful to every generation.
You hear the cry of barren hearts,

you bless the struggle in the womb,

you call nations from the wrestling of kin.

Your purposes move even through our conflict,

and your promise outlasts our grasping.
You are the God of generations and eternity,
      present in all our temporality and frailty.
So, teach us to live between the generations with humility.
Let us bless what came before
      and nurture what is yet to be.
Give us grace to reconcile what divides us,
      and faith to see that your covenant continues
            through imperfect heirs.
Make us keepers of memory and midwives of promise,
      people who hold both sorrow and hope without losing heart.
Until every rivalry yields to peace,
      until every inheritance becomes gift,
      until the generations walk together in light,
      until all reconciliation is complete in Christ,
      keep us faithful to your story.
Blessed are you, Ancient and Ever-New,
      who calls each generation by name.
Blessed are you, Christ our lineage of mercy.
Blessed are you, Spirit of promise,
      who renews the earth with every birth.
Amen.

Wells in a Dry Land (Genesis 26)

God of the living water,

    you sustain your people in famine,

    meeting us in brokenness and barrenness,

    you bless the fields of exiles,

    you make room where others would shut the gates.

We confess our fear of scarcity.

We hoard what could be shared,

    we dig our wells with suspicion,

    we exclude rather than welcome and embrace,

    we claim what was meant to sustain all.

Our faith shrinks when drought comes,

    our trust falters when others prosper.

We lament the quarrels that fill our valleys,

    neighbors fighting for water,

    nations tightening their fists around rivers and trade,

    hearts hardened by appetites and nationalisms,

    communities divided by envy.

We mourn the deep thirst of creation:

    the land cracked by greed,

    the hearts hardened by mistrust.

Yet you, O Lord, keep digging new beginnings.

You lead Isaac to Rehoboth,

    to wide places where there is room for all.

You show us that blessing isn't competition,

    but overflow.

So, unstop our wells, God of life.

Cleanse us of resentment and fear.

Teach us to draw from your abundance,

> to dig again where others have ceased to hope,
>
> to name each spring as gift, not prize.

Let our communities become oases,

> workplaces that refresh rather than drain,
>
> churches that welcome rather than guard,
>
> hearts that give rather than grasp,
>
> homes where reconciliation flows like rain,
>
> offering living waters from the springs of life flowing
>
> from the divine love of Father, Son, and Spirit.

Until every thirst is quenched,

> until peace runs through the furrows of the earth,
>
> until the nations drink together without fear,
>
> keep us near the source.

Blessed are you, Wellspring of mercy,

> who gives water in the desert.

Blessed are you, Christ our living stream,

> who reconciles those divided by drought.

Blessed are you, Spirit of renewal,

> who makes dry ground bloom again.

Amen.

The Stolen Blessing (Genesis 27)

God of tangled families and wounded love,
    you see through disguises,
    you hear what's whispered behind closed doors,
    you know the hearts that scheme and the hearts that break.
We confess our hunger to be blessed.
We clutch for affirmation,
    we steal what was meant to be shared,
    we dress in the garments of others to be seen and loved.
Our deceit wounds those we love most,
    and our craving blinds us to your abundance.
We lament a world shaped by rivalry,
    siblings estranged,
    generations divided by resentment,
    communities poisoned by competition.
We grieve that blessing has become a zero-sum game,
    where one must lose for another to gain.
Yet you, O Lord, weave mercy through our mess.
You don't discard the deceiver or the deceived.
You redeem the stolen word,
    turning even deceit into strange beginnings of grace.
So, unmask us, O God.
Strip away the false names we wear.
Teach us to bless without fear of scarcity,
    to trust that your favor is wider than our grasp.
Give us the courage to face those we've wronged,
    and the humility to seek forgiveness.

Make us a people who bless rather than compete,
  who tell truth instead of shaping lies,
  who find healing in the light of your steadfast love.
Until every household is reconciled,
  until blessings overflow without limit,
  until your truth restores what deceit destroyed,
  keep us near your mercy.
Blessed are you, God who redeems the deceivers,
  who turns fraud into grace.
Blessed are you, Christ our truth,
  whose blessing none can steal.
Blessed are you, Spirit of peace,
  who heals what lies have torn apart.
Amen.

The Ladder and the Stone (Genesis 28)

God of thresholds and hidden stairways,
>you meet wanderers in the wilderness,
>you speak in dreams to the fearful,
>you meet us where we are,
>with your holiness, love, and grace,
>you make ordinary ground shimmer with glory.

We confess how small our vision has become.
We divide life into sacred and secular,
>worship and work, heaven and earth.

We forget that you are present in every place,
>that angels still ascend and descend,
>that your presence is all around us,
>in the midst of our exhaustion and uncertainty.

We lament the loneliness of exile,
>those far from home or welcome,
>those sleeping on cold ground with nothing but stone for comfort,
>those sleeping rough without family or home,
>and the way we've contributed to systems that cause suffering.

We grieve for the dreamless,
>for those who can no longer imagine a world visited by your love.

Yet you, O Lord, still stand beside us.
You promise presence before provision,
>companionship before certainty,
>grace before plans,
>and renewal of our hearts and your earth.

You name yourself the God who won't leave us,

who guards our journeys and guides our return.
So, open our eyes to the ladders you've already placed before us,
>the small kindnesses, the moments of awe,
>
>the surprising nearness of your Spirit,
>
>the touch of empathy and humanity,
>
>the way creation signs of your presence and glory.

Teach us to build altars from the stones of our weariness,
>to mark our nights with gratitude rather than fear.

Make us pilgrims who see holiness in the ordinary,
>who trust that every wilderness hides revelation,
>
>who wake declaring, "Surely God is in this place."

Until the earth and heaven are one,
>until every exile finds home,
>
>until all creation and humanity sing your praise,
>
>until the gate of glory stands open for all,
>
>keep us dreaming in your light.

Blessed are you, God of Jacob,
>who turns fugitives into worshipers.

Blessed are you, Christ our ladder,
>who joins heaven and earth in mercy.

Blessed are you, Spirit of awe,
>who wakes us to wonder again.

Blessed are Father, Son, and Spirit,
>who restore all creation and humanity to relationship with you.

Amen.

Love by the Well, Tears at Night (Genesis 29)

God who meets us beside the wells of longing,
    you see the hearts that labor for love,
    you watch the weary under unfair hands,
    you remember those overlooked and unloved.
We confess our complicity in systems of exploitation.
We trade affection for advantage,
    we measure worth by beauty or productivity,
    we keep others working for what should be freely given.
We disguise manipulation as romance,
    and mistake control for devotion.
We lament those trapped in cycles of deceit,
    the Leahs unseen in a world chasing Rachels,
    the laborers who sweat for promises never kept,
    the dreamers still waiting for tenderness.
We lament this world of manipulation, exploitation, and pain,
    and the way our social and economic systems feed these things.
We grieve how often love itself becomes a transaction,
    and hope wears out before the harvest.
Yet you, O Lord, are faithful through the tangle.
You bless the unloved with fruitfulness,
    you weave your covenant through human frailty,
    you turn tears into the seedbed of promise.
So, redeem our affections, O God.
Teach us to love without possession,
    to work without resentment,
    to see beauty in those the world ignores.

Make our relationships wells of mercy,
>   not battlegrounds of desire.
Help us love and serve in a self-giving, generous way,
>   laying aside grasping and self-interest.
Let your justice re-order what deception has disfigured.
Let kindness become our currency,
>   and mutuality our labor of faith.
Until every Leah knows she is chosen,
>   until every weary worker rests in dignity,
>   until love flows freely as living water,
>   keep us faithful in your covenant of compassion.
We bless you our God, who loves and sees all people.
Blessed are you, God who sees the unloved,
>   who sanctifies even the night of disappointment.
Blessed are you, Christ our beloved,
>   who labors for our redemption.
Blessed are you, Spirit of tenderness,
>   who teaches hearts to love as you love.
Amen.

The God Who Remembers (Genesis 30)

God of life that refuses despair,
> you hear the cries of the barren and the bitter,
> you see the grasping and the grief,
> you remain faithful when our faith grows small.

We confess the envy that corrodes our souls.
We measure blessing by comparison,
> resenting what others receive,
> turning gift into grievance.

We scheme to manufacture what only grace can give,
> and in our striving, we forget to rest in you.

We lament the rivalries that divide your people,
> siblings at war for affection,
> families competing for love,
> churches opposing other churches,
> theological colleges acting like business competitors,
> nations clutching for dominance.

We mourn the wounds caused by jealousy,
> the exhaustion of endless striving,
> the silence that falls when compassion runs dry.

Yet you, O Lord, are the God who remembers.
You open wombs long closed,
> you breathe vitality into desolate hearts,
> you turn rivalry into redemption,
> you show us the meaning of self-giving love,
> you lead us away from grasping and competition,
> and reveal a new way on the Cross.

You bless not because we earn it,
>   but because love won't stop creating.
So quiet our comparisons,
>   loosen our grasp,
>   and teach us to trust your timing.
Let gratitude become our posture,
>   and joy our resistance to envy.
Help us celebrate another's blessing
>   as proof of your abundance, not our lack.
Make our households places of mutual delight,
>   our communities gardens of generosity,
>   our work the labor of shared hope,
>   our lives cruciform.
Until rivalry yields to rejoicing,
>   until barrenness sings with new life,
>   until your compassion renews all creation,
>   keep us faithful to your remembering love.
Blessed are you, God who opens what we have closed.
Blessed are you, Christ our fullness,
>   who frees us from envy's chains.
Blessed are you, Spirit of life,
>   who makes every barren field bloom again.
Amen.

Crossing the Threshold (Genesis 31)

God of the turning road,

 you speak in dreams and restlessness,

 you call the weary to leave what once sustained them,

 you discern plans for us way beyond our imaginings,

 you guide us through the ache of change toward freedom.

We confess how long we linger in places that no longer give life.

We mistake comfort for calling,

 we settle beneath the expectations of others,

 we cling to patterns that keep us small.

When you say "Go," we bargain for delay.

We lament the conflicts that haunt our leaving,

 broken covenants, unpaid debts,

 relationships strained by fear and pride,

 unforgiveness instead of grace,

 words spoken in anger or pride.

We grieve the mistrust that divides kin and community,

 the suspicion that poisons every negotiation,

 the way our sinfulness makes relationships transactional.

Yet you, O Lord, travel with the fugitives.

You are present with us in the liminal spaces.

You defend the wronged without weapon or wealth,

 you restrain wrath and expose deceit,

 you turn escape into pilgrimage and endings into beginnings.

So teach us to listen when you stir unrest.

Give us courage to rise, to gather what matters, to go.

Keep us honest when fear tempts us to cunning,

gentle when anger burns too hot,

    faithful when the path feels fragile.

Let reconciliation follow in our wake,

    and gratitude mark the borders we cross.

Make our journeys sanctuaries of your presence,

    tents of trust pitched in uncertain lands.

Until every exile finds rest,

    until old wounds are mended,

    until your wandering people know they're home,

    keep us moving in your mercy.

Blessed are you, God of the road,

    who guards travelers and redeems departures.

Blessed are you, Christ our companion,

    who walks beside the uncertain.

Blessed are you, Spirit of peace,

    who writes courage on weary, frightened, trembling hearts.

Amen.

The Wrestler's Blessing (Genesis 32)

God who meets us in the dark,
>   you come not as comfort but as struggle,
>   not to destroy but to transform,
>   not with answers but with presence.
We confess how much we avoid the night.
We fill our silence with noise,
>   our fear with bravado,
>   our loneliness with distraction.
We run from confrontation,
>   with others, with ourselves, with you.
We lament the violence within and around us,
>   our need to win,
>   our refusal to yield,
>   our complicity in systems that injure and oppress,
>   the harm we cause in defending our illusions.
We grieve the nights of terror and anxiety,
>   when every shadow feels like judgment.
Yet you, O Lord, wrestle us into truth.
You don't let go until we face ourselves.
You wound us with mercy,
>   so we may walk differently into the dawn.
You rename us,
>   and in that name, we are known and made new.
So meet us again at the river's edge.
Let our prayer become honest struggle,
>   our struggle become communion.

Teach us that blessing isn't escape,

> but the limp that reminds us of love's encounter.

Make us a people marked by grace,

> strong enough to yield,

> humble enough to bless even our enemies,

> open enough to live with ambiguity and uncertainty,

> courageous enough to walk into reconciliation.

Until every night gives way to morning,

> until every exile crosses home,

> until all striving ends in your embrace,

> keep us wrestling toward your peace.

Blessed are you, God of the night and the dawn,

> who turns fear into faith.

Blessed are you, Christ our companion in the struggle,

> whose wounds are our healing.

Blessed are you, Spirit of the breath and the river,

> who names us beloved again.

Amen.

Faces of Reconciliation (Genesis 33)

God of mended roads,
>you guide trembling feet toward old wounds,
>you teach the proud to bow,
>you make forgiveness possible in the soil of fear.

We confess how long we carry grudges.
We rehearse grievances until they become our identity,
>we keep score of every slight,
>we avoid the hard road back to those we've hurt.

Our pride disguises itself as dignity,
>but it only keeps us lonely.

We lament the estrangements that define our world,
>siblings who no longer speak,
>neighbors divided by history,
>peoples locked in vengeance,
>partisan politics that divides us,
>violent ethnic and cultural enmities.

We mourn how easily our wounds justify our weapons,
>and how mercy seems naïve in the age of outrage.

Yet you, O Lord, go before us on the road of return.
You soften Esau's heart before Jacob arrives.
You turn fear into embrace,
>you make faces radiant again with recognition.

You reveal yourself in the one we feared to meet.
So humble us, O God.
Let reconciliation begin in us.
Give us courage to take the first step,

to speak truth without blame,
to offer and receive forgiveness as gift,
to embrace those who've been our enemies,
to see the humanity in those we've objectified,
to love our enemies as Christ commands.
Make our communities spaces of restored kinship,
tables where enemies eat together,
streets where history is healed,
families where love outruns resentment.
Until every exile is welcomed,
until every conflict yields to peace,
until we see your face in one another,
keep us walking the road of mercy.
Blessed are you, God of reconciliation,
who breaks the power of revenge.
Blessed are you, Christ our peace,
who meets us in the face of the other.
Blessed are you, Spirit of tenderness,
who reconciles estranged hearts into one family.
Until all relationships are reconciled,
and you restore all creation and humanity to shalom,
and relationship with you.
Amen.

The Cry No One Heard (Genesis 34)

God of the violated and unheard,

    you gather the broken into your arms,

    you grieve what we'd rather forget,

    you hear the cries that human power silences.

We confess our complicity in cultures of violence.

We look away from suffering,

    we protect reputations instead of the wounded,

    we confuse vengeance with justice.

Too often, we use your name to bless domination,

    and call silence peace.

We lament the story of Dinah,

    a daughter defiled, a family enraged,

    a city drenched in retaliatory blood.

We lament every victim whose story is buried,

    every survivor dismissed as inconvenience,

    every act of revenge that deepens the wound.

The ground itself groans beneath the weight of it all.

Yet you, O Lord, don't turn away.

You dwell among the shamed and forsaken.

You name truth where others deny it.

You hold the violated with tenderness,

    and expose the hypocrisy of the powerful.

So teach us your holy justice,

    the justice that restores, not destroys,

    that defends the vulnerable and dismantles cruelty.

Let our anger become compassion,

our sorrow become solidarity,

      our silence give way to truth.

Make your church a refuge, not a court of fear.

Let every Dinah find safety and dignity among your people.

Teach us to heal without hatred,

      to remember without revenge.

Until all violence ends,

      until every wound is mended,

      until tears are wiped from every face,

      keep us faithful to your fierce mercy.

Blessed are you, God who hears what others ignore,

      who gathers justice and gentleness in one hand.

Blessed are you, Christ our wounded healer,

      whose scars speak truth.

Blessed are you, Spirit of comfort,

      who restores what evil tried to erase.

Amen.

Return and Renewal (Genesis 35)

God of second beginnings,

    you call us back to the places where promise was first spoken,

    you wait for us at altars we once built and abandoned,

    you invite us to start again, not by erasing the past,

    but by redeeming it.

We confess the idols we've carried too long,

    our fears disguised as control,

    our grudges dressed as wisdom,

    our habits of convenience and despair.

We cling to what once comforted but now corrodes.

We've forgotten how to travel light.

Help us to topple the gods of money and success,

    teach us instead the wealth of generosity and the joy of enough.

Unmask the idols of comfort and control,

    show us the wild freedom of trust and surrender.

Silence the false prophets of fame and image,

    let us live unfiltered and unafraid in your light.

Dismantle our devotion to productivity and perfection,

    teach us the sacred art of rest, the courage to be unfinished.

Free us from the altars of nation and tribe,

    form us into a people whose loyalty is love.

Unplug us from the glowing screens of distraction,

    draw us back to the stillness where your voice can be heard.

Heal us of our worship of youth and beauty,

    teach us to honor wrinkles as testimonies of grace.

Deliver us from our obsession with safety and power,

make us daring in mercy and generous in peace.
And save us, Lord, from the idol that bears your name,
    the religion of self-righteousness that forgets compassion.
Break every chain that keeps us from your likeness,
    until our hearts bow only to you,
    the God who is love,
    the Lord who is enough.
We lament the weight of what we drag behind us,
    false gods and idols we refuse to release.
We grieve how rarely we stop to build altars,
    to name gratitude,
    to remember mercy.
Yet you, O Lord, summon us to Bethel again.
You remind us that grace still dwells where we first believed.
You tell us to bury the idols beneath the oak,
    to wash, to change our garments,
    to rise and worship.
You transform places of fear into gateways of peace.
So lead us back, O God.
Let us mark our journey with remembrance and release.
Give us courage to lay down what enslaves us,
    and faith to carry only your promise forward.
Make our lives living altars,
    stones of truth,
    offerings of gratitude,
    monuments of reconciliation.
Until every idol is buried,
    until every home becomes Bethel,
    until your name is praised in every heart,
    keep us returning to your mercy.
Blessed are you, God of renewal,
    who calls wanderers home.
Blessed are you, Christ our altar,

who sanctifies the ordinary.
Blessed are you, Spirit of cleansing,
who turns burial into birth.
Amen.

The Forgotten Genealogies (Genesis 36)

God of every lineage and story,

  you remember the names history forgets,

  you trace your mercy through bloodlines and brokenness,

  you show grace through the faith and doubt of families
  throughout generations,

  you see the worth of those the world deems irrelevant.

We confess how easily we overlook what seems ordinary.

We rush through the lists,

  we skip the names we can't pronounce,

  we ignore the stories that seem old or irrelevant,

  we measure importance by influence and fame.

We forget that every life,

  every generation,

  is a thread in your story of love and grace.

We lament a culture obsessed with pedigree and visibility,

  where some are idolized and others erased,

  where ancestry becomes pride or shame,

  where the unknown live and die without record or honor.

We mourn how often we claim your blessing for ourselves

  and forget your faithfulness extends to others too.

Yet you, O Lord, are the keeper of names.

You write every story into your book of life.

You bless Esau as well as Jacob,

  you fill the earth with tribes and tongues,

  you remind us that your covenant overflows its boundaries.

So teach us to see holiness in the overlooked.

Help us honor the long faithfulness of families,

    the steady endurance of generations who till the soil,

    raise their children,

    and keep your ways unseen.

Let gratitude deepen our memory,

    and humility widen our belonging.

Make us tell stories that restore dignity,

    build communities that cherish every name,

    and speak blessings that include rather than exclude.

Until all nations are remembered,

    until every name is spoken with love,

    until your great family is gathered as one,

    keep us faithful to your remembering.

Blessed are you, God of generations,

    who forgets no name.

Blessed are you, Christ our brother,

    who gathers every lineage into grace.

Blessed are you, Spirit of memory,

    who joins our small stories into your eternal one.

Amen.

Dreams in the Pit (Genesis 37)

God of dreams and disappointments,
>you speak to the young in visions,
>you plant hope in the hearts of the overlooked,
>you work your will through stories that begin in pain.

We confess how quickly we envy the dreamers.
We mock what we don't understand,
>we resent those whose hope unsettles our despair,
>we tear down what threatens our control.

Too often we trade wonder for cynicism
>and call it maturity.

We lament the cruelty of jealousy,
>brothers who plot against brothers,
>families who turn love into rivalry,
>communities that crush their visionaries.

We grieve the pits we dig for others,
>the dismissals, the betrayals, the silences,
>and the pits we find ourselves in
>when the world feels indifferent to our own dreams.

Yet you, O Lord, aren't absent from the depths.
You travel with the betrayed,
>you turn slave roads into pathways of promise,
>you whisper destiny through tears.

No pit is beyond your redemption,
>no dream too fragile for your breath.

So keep alive in us the courage to dream again.
Give us faith to endure misunderstanding,

patience when your timing feels cruel,

and grace to bless even those who wound us.

Make us protectors of vision,

nurturers of possibility,

people who refuse to bury hope.

Until every pit becomes a well of living water,

until the dreamers rise to heal the nations,

until your purpose outlasts our malice,

keep us faithful to the dreams you give.

Blessed are you, God of the pit and the promise,

who remembers the forgotten.

Blessed are you, Christ our dream made flesh,

who redeems betrayal with love.

Blessed are you, Spirit of vision,

who keeps hope alive in the dark.

Amen.

The Righteous Outcast (Genesis 38)

God of hidden justice,
>you see the ones cast aside by power,
>
>you vindicate the shamed and silenced,
>
>you bring truth to light through those the world forgets.

We confess our complicity in Tamar's story.

We have ignored the cries of those mistreated,
>dismissed women's courage as defiance,
>
>and hidden behind laws that protect privilege.

We have feared scandal more than injustice,
>and called silence virtue when it served our comfort.

We lament every Tamar still waiting for vindication,
>those exploited and disbelieved,
>
>those left without protection or name,
>
>those punished for demanding fairness.

We grieve the hypocrisy that still cloaks abuse in righteousness,
>and the systems that favor the powerful
>>while shaming the wounded.

Yet you, O Lord, are the defender of the wronged.

You don't forget the brave or the broken.

You write Tamar's name into the lineage of redemption.

You expose deceit and call the outcast righteous.

You show that holiness sometimes wears the face of defiance.

So awaken our courage, God of truth.

Teach us to stand with the accused,
>to listen before judging,
>
>to risk our reputation for the sake of the oppressed.

Let your justice be the measure of our faith,
>and compassion the proof of our holiness.

Make your church a refuge where dignity is restored,
>where shame has no voice,
>and truth finds safety to speak.

Until righteousness rolls down like waters,
>until no Tamar stands alone,
>until your mercy rewrites every story,
>keep us faithful to your justice.

Blessed are you, God of the fearless and the forgotten,
>who overturns hypocrisy with grace.

Blessed are you, Christ our Redeemer,
>born of Tamar's courage.

Blessed are you, Spirit of truth,
>who vindicates the silenced.

Amen.

Faithful in the Shadows (Genesis 39)

God who is present in every exile,

    you were with Joseph in the house of power,

    you were with him in the prison's dark,

    you were with him when his reputation was maligned,

    you were with him when he suffered,

    you are with all who walk faithfully yet suffer for their truth.

We confess how quickly we compromise.

We bend truth to advantage,

    we excuse ourselves for what convenience demands,

    we trade integrity for approval.

We hide our convictions when they cost too much.

We lament a world where innocence is punished,

    where the honest are slandered,

    where whistle-blowers are attacked,

    where manipulation triumphs over honor,

    where those without power bear the blame of the powerful.

We grieve the long silences of injustice,

    the forgotten cells where the faithful wait for dawn.

Yet you, O Lord, never leave the imprisoned heart.

Your presence is light in the deepest dungeon.

You prosper righteousness even when it seems defeated.

You turn false accusation into the seed of deliverance.

In the places of confinement, your kingdom quietly grows.

So steady us when integrity isolates us.

Give us courage to resist temptation,

    grace to endure misunderstanding,

and faith to trust your unseen work.
Let your Spirit strengthen those falsely accused,
>	and your mercy defend those without defense.
Make us a people who guard conscience more than comfort,
>	who choose faithfulness over favor,
>	and who wait in hope, even when vindication seems far away.
Until every prison door opens,
>	until truth stands free and radiant,
>	until your justice restores all that lies broken,
>	keep us faithful in the shadows.
Blessed are you, God of the imprisoned and pure in heart,
>	who honors truth over triumph.
Blessed are you, Christ our companion in the cell,
>	who redeems what others meant for harm.
Blessed are you, Spirit of courage,
>	who keeps integrity alive in the dark.
Amen.

The Dreams of the Forgotten (Genesis 40)

God who listens in the stillness of forgotten places,
    you hear the sighs that never reach the surface,
    you keep faith with the imprisoned dreamer,
    you remember what others neglect.
We confess how restless we grow in waiting.
We want rescue on demand,
    we measure your presence by our progress,
    we mistake delay for abandonment.
We serve faithfully, yet crave recognition,
    forgetting that unseen faithfulness still shines in your eyes.
We lament the long years of obscurity,
    the labor unnoticed,
    the prayers unanswered,
    the hope deferred until hearts grow heavy.
We grieve a world that forgets its servants,
    that uses gifts when convenient
    and discards people when their usefulness fades.
Yet you, O Lord, dwell in the shadows.
You breathe meaning into our hidden labor.
You turn forgotten prisons into schools of wisdom.
You weave redemption quietly, thread by unseen thread,
    until the forgotten moment becomes the doorway of promise.
So teach us to dream again in the waiting.
Let patience become our prayer,
    and faithfulness our protest against despair.
Keep us gentle when disappointment tempts us to bitterness,

and grateful when small mercies arrive.
Make us companions to those who wait without recognition,
    interpreters of hope in desolate rooms,
    people whose presence reminds others they aren't alone.
Until every dream is remembered,
    until every servant stands vindicated,
    until the cell becomes the threshold of freedom,
    keep us steadfast in your love.
Blessed are you, Keeper of forgotten dreams,
    who remembers every sigh.
Blessed are you, Christ our hidden companion,
    whose silence is full of promise.
Blessed are you, Spirit of remembrance,
    who turns delay into deliverance.
Amen.

Bread for the Nations (Genesis 41)

God of the long arc of waiting,
>you lift dreamers from prisons to palaces,
>you give wisdom not for status but for service,
>you feed the world through those who have learned to hunger.

We confess how easily success seduces us.
We mistake position for purpose,
>we hoard abundance while others starve,
>we call privilege providence.

We forget the famine beyond our gates
>and the humility that opened them.

We lament a world ruled by appetite,
>storehouses full while children faint,
>leaders deaf to wisdom unless it flatters them,
>systems that reward fear and punish imagination.

We mourn that our prosperity so often costs another's bread.
Yet you, O Lord, still raise Josephs in every age.
You teach discernment in the shadows,
>you entrust power to the tested,
>you turn dreams into policies of mercy.

Through the steady hands of the faithful,
>you keep the world from collapse.

So grant us the wisdom that serves rather than rules.
Teach us to plan with compassion,
>to steward abundance as belonging to all,
>to listen for your Spirit in the councils of power.

Let gratitude temper authority,

and justice guide every decision.
Make us bakers of hope in a starving land,
      hands that distribute rather than clutch,
      hearts that remember the pit even from the throne.
Until every table is filled,
      until wisdom governs with love,
      until the earth itself is satisfied with your goodness,
      keep us humble in plenty and steadfast in mercy.
Blessed are you, God of grain and grace,
      who remembers the hungry.
Blessed are you, Christ our bread of life,
      who feeds both body and soul.
Blessed are you, Spirit of wisdom,
      who teaches power to serve.
Amen.

The Hunger That Remembers (Genesis 42)

God who sends both famine and mercy,
>you shake our comfort so that truth may rise,
>you awaken memory through hunger,
>you call estranged hearts toward reconciliation long delayed.

We confess the sins we've buried deep.
We cover our guilt with busyness and pride,
>we silence conscience with denial,
>we pretend that distance is peace.

Yet old wounds keep speaking,
>and our hunger exposes what we tried to forget.

We lament a world starved of compassion,
>nations guarding grain instead of sharing it,
>families divided by shame and silence,
>souls numbed by luxury while others die in want.

We grieve how easily we justify indifference,
>how long it takes us to say, "We were wrong."

Yet you, O Lord, work even through famine.
You turn scarcity into invitation,
>you use longing to lead us home.

In the strange face of Joseph's authority
>you begin the hard mercy of recognition.

So feed us, God of truth.
Give us courage to face what we've denied,
>grace to confess without excuse,
>and humility to seek the forgiveness we once withheld.

Let hunger become our teacher,

and repentance our harvest.

Make us generous in a world of guarded storehouses,

    willing to give what we hoarded,

    ready to mend what we fractured.

Until estranged brothers embrace,

    until every table becomes a place of grace,

    until famine ends in feast,

    keep us hungry for your mercy.

Blessed are you, God who remembers the guilty with compassion.

Blessed are you, Christ our bread in famine,

    who feeds repentance with love.

Blessed are you, Spirit of restoration,

    who turns hunger into healing.

Amen.

The Table of Return (Genesis 43)

God of second journeys,
>   you call us back to places we fled in fear,
>   you turn necessity into grace,
>   you have plans for us more redemptive than we know,
>   you prepare tables where estranged hearts may meet again.

We confess our reluctance to return.
We prefer distance to honesty,
>   excuses to confession,
>   control to vulnerability.

We fear mercy's exposure,
>   and suspect that forgiveness might ask too much.

We lament the long cold between brothers and kin,
>   families fractured by old stories,
>   nations built on suspicion,
>   love withheld until it's too late.

We mourn how rarely we risk tenderness,
>   how easily we armor ourselves against reconciliation.

Yet you, O Lord, arrange the meal.
You set Joseph's table for those who once sold him,
>   you fill empty sacks with abundance,
>   you hide silver in the grain of grace.

You turn famine into fellowship,
>   and guilt into the doorway of peace.

So teach us to sit again where hurt began.
Make our tables wide with mercy,
>   our hearts ready for surprise.

Give us courage to return without pretense,
　　to receive kindness we no longer expect,
　　to believe that reconciliation is still possible.
Let generosity break the power of fear,
　　and hospitality undo the logic of vengeance.
Let shared bread become the language of healing.
Until every estrangement ends in embrace,
　　until every wound becomes a scar of peace,
　　until the feast of your kingdom gathers all,
　　keep us returning in hope.
Blessed are you, God of the open table,
　　who feeds the guilty with grace.
Blessed are you, Christ our host,
　　who turns enemies into guests.
Blessed are you, Spirit of reconciliation,
　　who writes forgiveness into our shared bread.
Amen.

The Cup of Truth (Genesis 44)

God who searches hearts without cruelty,
    you uncover what deceit has buried,
    you test not to shame but to heal,
    you bring truth into the light so that mercy may endure.
We confess how we hide behind appearances.
We speak half-truths to survive,
    we justify small betrayals,
    we protect ourselves at the cost of others.
We want forgiveness without the risk of exposure.
We lament a world allergic to confession,
    leaders who won't not admit fault,
    families fractured by secrets,
    souls afraid to be known.
We grieve how easily we trade honesty for control,
    and how healing eludes us because we cling to our masks.
Yet you, O Lord, are gentle in your unveiling.
Through Joseph's testing, you awaken remorse.
Through Judah's plea, love remembers its brother.
You show us that confession isn't humiliation
    but the doorway to reconciliation.
So search us, God of truth.
Expose what we've concealed;
    not to wound, but to free.
Teach us to own our wrongs without despair,
    to offer restitution where we can,
    to trust that your mercy is stronger than our guilt.

Let truth become our language,

and compassion the measure of our courage.

Let repentance bind us closer,

and integrity mark your people's way.

Until deception is no longer needed,

until every wrong is faced and forgiven,

until love restores what shame divided,

keep us honest in your light.

Blessed are you, God of the searching heart,

who reveals without destroying.

Blessed are you, Christ our truth,

who bears our exposure with grace.

Blessed are you, Spirit of gentleness,

who turns confession into freedom.

Amen.

The Embrace of Grace (Genesis 45)

God of reconciliation and wonder,
>you make tears holy,
>you turn years of silence into a single moment of mercy,
>you bring estranged hearts together
>>until they dawn with recognition.

We confess how long we withhold forgiveness.
We rehearse old injuries until they harden,
>we cling to wounds that have become part of our identity,
>we fear that reconciliation will cost too much.

We want resurrection without surrender,
>healing without truth.

We lament the chasms between us,
>families divided by pride,
>communities scarred by prejudice,
>nations trapped in cycles of revenge.

We grieve the suffering of those who wait for an apology
>>that never comes,
>and the arrogance of those who think mercy weakness.

Yet you, O Lord, bring brothers to embrace in Egypt.
You turn famine into feast,
>betrayal into reunion,
>remorse into rejoicing.

You show us that forgiveness isn't forgetting,
>but the miracle of love stronger than memory.

So break our defenses with tenderness.
Let tears become our prayer when words fail.

Give us courage to reveal ourselves and to receive others' truth.
Make our compassion larger than our pain,
 and our hope deeper than our history.
Let reconciliation be the fruit of your Spirit among us,
 justice kissed with kindness,
 mercy woven into every conversation,
 peace born from shared tears.
Until all divisions end in embrace,
 until every exile comes home,
 until love's weeping fills the earth with joy,
 keep us open to your reconciling grace.
Blessed are you, God of the long-awaited embrace,
 who writes forgiveness into history.
Blessed are you, Christ our peace,
 whose tears redeem the world.
Blessed are you, Spirit of mercy,
 who makes enemies kin again.
Amen.

The Journey into Egypt (Genesis 46)

God of thresholds and promises kept,
    you call us to go where memory trembles,
    you lead us into foreign lands that will shape our future,
    you walk beside us when our steps are slow with age and grief.
We confess how hard it is to leave what is known.
We cling to the familiar even when it no longer gives life.
We fear change disguised as calling,
    and prefer nostalgia to faith.
Our trust falters when obedience leads us into uncertainty.
We lament the migrations that tear families apart,
    those fleeing war, famine, or despair,
    the elders left behind, the children growing up between worlds.
We mourn the losses hidden in every new beginning,
    the languages forgotten, the graves left untended.
Yet you, O Lord, meet Jacob in the night of departure.
You speak his name with tenderness,
    you promise presence in the unknown,
    you assure him that Egypt, too, can become holy ground.
You are God not of one place, but of the journey itself.
So go with us, O Faithful Companion.
Carry our fears as we cross uncertain borders.
Make our going an act of trust,
    and our arriving an act of praise.
Let your mercy travel with every migrant and pilgrim,
    and your Spirit build home wherever your people dwell.
Make our hearts hospitable,

our communities sanctuaries of welcome,
    our memories wells of gratitude, not regret.
Until every exile is gathered,
    until every journey finds its rest,
    until your dwelling fills all creation,
    keep us moving in your promise.
Blessed are you, God of the road and the homeland,
    who calls us by name in every land.
Blessed are you, Christ our companion,
    who makes the strange place home.
Blessed are you, Spirit of pilgrimage,
    who guides us still.
Amen.

Wisdom in a Famine (Genesis 47)

God of justice and provision,
    you plant wisdom in unlikely hearts,
    you teach compassion in the courts of kings,
    you call your people to sustain life
        even inside the machinery of empire.
We confess our compromises with power.
We barter truth for influence,
    mistake ambition for calling,
    and confuse management with mercy.
We hoard when you invite us to share,
    forgetting that abundance becomes idolatry
        when it stops serving love.
We lament the famines still devouring the earth,
    bellies empty in lands of surplus,
    the poor sold their own freedom to survive,
    policies written to protect the wealthy
        while others waste away.
We grieve our comfort in a world of hunger,
    and the systems we perpetuate to keep it that way.
Yet you, O Lord, are present even in Pharaoh's halls.
You give Joseph discernment to steward rather than exploit,
    to feed instead of rule.
You turn bureaucracy into blessing,
    and famine into the theater of grace.
So teach us to lead as servants,
    to wield influence with humility,

to let justice, not profit, set our measures.
Make us people whose wisdom shelters the vulnerable,
    whose generosity disrupts oppression.
Let our communities become storehouses of mercy,
    where none are shamed for need,
    and every gift is shared for the common good.
Until every famine ends in fullness,
    until no one sells dignity for bread,
    until your kingdom's equity fills the earth,
    keep us faithful stewards of your abundance.
Blessed are you, God of enough,
    who feeds the hungry with wisdom.
Blessed are you, Christ our sustainer,
    who redefines power as service.
Blessed are you, Spirit of generosity,
    who multiplies compassion like grain.
Amen.

The Crossed Hands of Blessing (Genesis 48)

God of memory and mercy,
>you dwell in the stories we tell at the edge of our lives,
>you are the Keeper of promises,
>the One who blesses beyond human logic or order.

We confess our obsession with control.
We cling to the firstborn privileges of power and certainty,
>we measure worth by sequence and status,
>we expect your blessing to follow our rules.

We forget that grace delights in surprise.
We lament how easily we weaponize inheritance,
>passing down prejudice instead of promise,
>fear instead of faith.

We mourn the hierarchies we build to protect ourselves,
>and the children who inherit our anxieties instead of our trust.

Yet you, O Lord, cross your hands.
You bless the younger before the elder,
>you rewrite the script of entitlement,
>you make mercy your lineage.

Your hands confound our expectations
>and remind us that love chooses freely.

So teach us to bless with open palms.
Let our prayers reach across divisions,
>our words speak life to the overlooked,
>our faith make room for surprise.

Help us pass on courage instead of comfort,
>grace instead of grievance,

hope instead of fear.

Make our households altars of blessing,

       our aging years testimonies of faithfulness,

       our memories seeds for the next generation's flourishing.

Until all boundaries of birth and status dissolve,

       until every child knows they are chosen,

       until your blessing fills the earth like light,

       keep our hands open to your unexpected grace.

Blessed are you, God of crossed hands,

       who subverts hierarchy with love.

Blessed are you, Christ our inheritance,

       whose mercy claims us all.

Blessed are you, Spirit of blessing,

       who makes the last first in joy.

Amen.

The Blessing and the Future (Genesis 49)

God of beginnings and endings,
> you gather families to speak truth before farewell,
> you turn old words into seeds of promise,
> you breathe blessing even through trembling voices.

We confess how poorly we handle endings.
We rush through partings,
> we avoid the honesty that love requires,
> we want comfort more than truth.

We forget that blessing costs something,
> a reckoning with what has been,
> and courage to release what must change.

We lament the patterns that pass unexamined
> from generation to generation,
> anger inherited like debt,
> favoritism disguised as affection,
> silence handed down as tradition.

We mourn the blessings withheld,
> the words never spoken,
> the reconciliation delayed until it's too late.

Yet you, O Lord, stand among the gathered.
You transform final words into prophecy.
You let truth be spoken,
> and grace hidden within the naming.

You remind us that every blessing, even mixed with frailty,
> can become soil for redemption.

So teach us to bless honestly.

Let our words heal without flattery,

 challenge without wounding,

 and plant hope where fear once ruled.

Give us courage to speak grace into the future

 and to trust that your Spirit will carry it onward.

Make our memories fertile with forgiveness,

 our farewells rich with peace,

 our legacies alive with love.

Until every generation knows itself beloved,

 until every story ends in mercy,

 until the final word is joy,

 keep us blessing in your name.

Blessed are you, God of every generation,

 who gathers the living and the dying in one embrace.

Blessed are you, Christ our inheritance of peace.

Blessed are you, Spirit of truth,

 who turns memory into promise.

Amen.

The Bones of Promise (Genesis 50)

God of endings that aren't the end,
> you receive our tears as offerings,
> you hold our grief with gentleness,
> you turn even death into the seed of new beginnings.
We confess our unease with mortality.
We hide from sorrow with distraction,
> we rush to tidy up grief before it finishes its work,
> we speak of heaven while fearing the grave.
We forget that mourning, too, is a sacred act of trust.
We lament the pain of parting,
> empty rooms and unfinished words,
> the ache of generations passing,
> the distance between those who remain
> and those gone before.
We mourn how often death reveals
> the fractures we refused to heal,
> how bitterness can outlive the body.
Yet you, O Lord, speak life even at the tomb.
You teach forgiveness in the wake of loss.
You gather Joseph and his brothers in mercy,
> you turn their guilt into grace.
You remind us that your covenant outlasts our frailty,
> that the bones we carry are promises, not relics.
So teach us to grieve with gratitude,
> to forgive while it is still called today,
> to honor the dead by loving the living well.

Let every burial be a sowing,

> and every tear a prayer of resurrection.

Make our faith as sturdy as Joseph's hope,

> who asked to be carried forward when freedom would come.

Let us live and die believing your word.

Until the graves are empty,

> until reunion replaces separation,

> until love's promise stands fulfilled,

> keep us steadfast in your mercy.

Blessed are you, Keeper of the covenant,

> who remembers dust and breath alike.

Blessed are you, Christ of the empty tomb,

> whose love conquers death.

Blessed are you, Spirit of consolation,

> who weaves sorrow into glory.

Amen.

From Dust to Promise: A Prayer for the Whole of Genesis

God of beginnings and becoming,
>you spoke the world from chaos into beauty,
>breathed life into dust,
>and called every creature good.

You walked with wanderers,
>remembered the barren,
>wrestled the proud,
>and stayed faithful to the faithless.

We confess how easily we forget our origin and calling.
We guard our own Edens instead of tending the world.
We build towers when you call us to pilgrimage,
>and trade your covenant for convenience.

We have lived as if the story were ours to control.
We lament the violence we inherit and perpetuate,
>the Cains who rise in every generation,
>the Pharaohs we serve with willing hearts,
>the fractures in families, nations, and souls.

The world still groans under the weight of our unmaking.
Yet you, O Lord, keep creating.
You speak light where darkness gathers,
>you find covenant partners in impossible places,
>you turn graves and wombs alike into gardens of hope.

You bless the barren,
>you remember the forgotten,
>you breathe again into those who thought their story over.

So teach us to live as children of Genesis,

> image-bearers who mend what we have broken,

> pilgrims who trust promise more than fear,

> peacemakers who remember the dust from which we came.

Make our work continuation, not possession;

> our prayers echoes of your creating love.

Let every ending remind us that the story continues in grace.

Until creation is healed,

> until every exile comes home,

> until your image shines in every face,

> keep us faithful to your beginning.

Blessed are you, Alpha of all things,

> whose breath still stirs the dust.

Blessed are you, Christ our covenant made flesh.

Blessed are you, Spirit of new creation,

> who makes all things possible again.

Amen.

Benediction: To Those Who Keep Beginning

Go now, children of dust and promise.

Walk in the light that still hovers over chaos.

Carry the breath that once stirred the first dawn.

Let your work join creation's unfinished song,

    planting, healing, forgiving, beginning again.

Remember the God who calls your name in every wilderness,

    who writes mercy into every ending,

    who blesses you to be a blessing.

Let your life become an altar of gratitude,

    your words a well for the thirsty,

    your presence a sign that grace endures.

And when the road feels long,

    remember: the Maker walks beside you still.

The Story has not ended.

The Spirit has not ceased to hover.

And even now, creation leans forward,

    waiting for your yes.

Go in peace,

    and keep beginning with God.

Amen.

Appendix 1: Would You Help?

Writing a book takes immense effort. It's a sustained labor of love over months, even years. Every page carries hours of thought, prayer, revision, and hope. And while the writing may be solitary, the life of a book is communal. That's where you come in. If this book has meant something to you, I'd be deeply grateful if you could help it find its way into more hands and hearts.

There are two simple but powerful ways you can do that.

First, consider leaving a short review on Amazon (and Goodreads would be wonderful too). Even just a few sentences can help others discover the book, as reviews significantly influence how books are recommended and shared online. You can do that by visiting Amazon or searching for this book and writing a review. Even a short note helps people find the book.

Second, if the book has stirred something in you, would you share it with others: friends, groups, churches, or anyone who might benefit from its message?

Your support helps keep this work going, and it means more than I can say. Thank you for being part of this journey.

Find this book on these pages:
1. Amazon:
https://www.amazon.com.au/stores/author/B008NI4ORQ
2. Goodreads:
https://www.goodreads.com/author/show/20347171.Graham_Joseph
_Hill
3. Author Website:

https://grahamjosephhill.com/books/

Appendix 2: About Me

Graham Joseph Hill (OAM, PhD) is an Adjunct Research Fellow and Associate Professor at Charles Sturt University, and one of Australia's most prolific and awarded Christian authors. He's written more than twenty books, including *Salt, Light, and a City*, which was named Jesus Creed's 2012 Book of the Year (church category); *Healing Our Broken Humanity* (with Grace Ji-Sun Kim), named Outreach Magazine's 2019 Resource of the Year (culture category); and *World Christianity*, shortlisted for the 2025 Australian Christian Book of the Year. In 2024, Graham was awarded the Medal of the Order of Australia (OAM) for his service to theological education. He lives in Sydney with his wife, Shyn.

Author and Ministry Websites

GrahamJosephHill.com

GrahamJosephHill.Substack.com

youtube.com/@GrahamJosephHill_Author

Linktr.ee/dailydevotions

facebook.com/grahamjosephhill/

instagram.com/grahamjosephhill/

amazon.com.au/stores/author/B008NI4ORQ

goodreads.com/author/show/20347171.Graham_Joseph_Hill

Books

See all my books at GrahamJosephHill.com/books

Appendix 3: Connect With Me

I'd love to stay connected with you. You can sign up to my Substack, Spirituality and Society with Hilly, where I share new writing, spiritual reflections, and updates on future books. Please find me on Substack: https://grahamjosephhill.substack.com

You can also find my books on my website: https://grahamjosephhill.com/books

You can also connect with me through my Facebook author page: https://www.facebook.com/GrahamJosephHill/

www.ingramcontent.com/pod-product-compliance
Lightning Source LLC
Chambersburg PA
CBHW031323040426

42443CB00005B/192